concerning

THE ATLAS OF SCOTLAND

and other poems

TOM POW

In Association with the National Library of Scotland

nls National Library of Scotland
Leabharlann Nàiseanta na h-Alba

Books by Tom Pow also published by Polygon

POETRY

A Wild Adventure, Thomas Watling, Dumfries Convict Artist
In The Becoming, New and Selected Poems

PROSE

In Another World, Among Europe's Dying Villages

FOR CHILDREN

When The Rains Con

First published in Great Britain in 2014 by Polygon, an imprint of Birlinn Ltd,
West Newington House, 10 Newington Road, Edinburgh EH9 1QS
www.polygonbooks.co.uk

ISBN: 978 1 84697 301 7
British Library Cataloguing-in-Publication Data
A catalogue record for this book is available on request from the British Library.

Design by Teresa Monachino.
Printed and bound in Spain at GraphyCems S.L.
by arrangement with Associated Agencies Oxford.

concerning
THE ATLAS OF SCOTLAND
and other poems

Poems written in response to experiences as the Bartholomew Writer in Residence at the National Library of Scotland, February–May 2013 – with illustrations drawn from collections at the National Library of Scotland and with drawings by Diane Garrick, Bartholomew Artist in Residence.

This book is for Cameron and Jenny

Blackburn   Wakefield   Rochdale   Preston   Lancaster   Workington

Aa Bb Cc Dd Ee Ff Gg Hh Ii Jj Kk Ll Mm Nn Oo Pp Qq

Rr Ss Tt Uu Vv Ww Xx Yy Zz   Caledonian Canal

Norwich   Lowestoft   Yarmouth   Colchester   Stratford on Avon   Bath e

Rugby   Oxford   Huntingdon   St Albans   Luton   Aylesbury   Tunbridge Wells   Ely

Forfar   Arbroath   Carnoustie   Rosyth   Kinghorn   Dunfermline   Crieff

Kendal   *Penrith*   Hawkshead   *Grasmere*   Whitehaven   *Northallerton*   Darlington   *Nottingham*

In the beginning was
THE MAP

CONTENTS

Each of our lives traces its own map onto the shared terrain.

BY REBECCA SOLNIT, A FIELD GUIDE TO GETTING LOST.

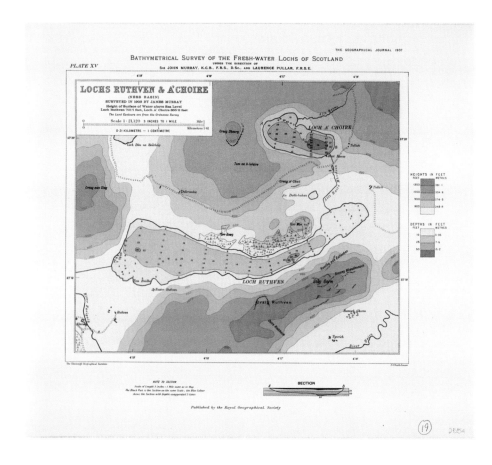

GEOGRAPHY

I was taught geography
by a man whose right eye
was a tiny globe of glass.

When he glanced to catch you
unawares, he fixed you
with one fierce blue eye

and stalled while the other
swivelled into place. It was
a first lesson in time zones.

BARTHOLOMEW MAP TITLE
*Map of Scotland to Illustrate
Mr Harvie Brown's Paper
on the Tufted Duck,* 1896

A PAIR OF LOCHS

Loch a'Choire

A skim of ruffled pewter.
A few reeds. Not much more.
Nor on the forestry track
that led to it – three straight

miles, the last with the loch-
keeper's squat cottage never
lost from sight. Somewhere,
our father's caught in a snap,

standing side on, pointing
stiffly at nothing much
with his birch walker's stick.
Even so, he held the pose,

long after the firs shot up
either side of the track –
enfolding him in shadow,
like the crags of Creag Dearg.

N
8 ← ✦ → 9

2 / 23

- -

BARTHOLOMEW MAP TITLE
Nobel's Explosives Company,
The British Empire on
Mercator's Projection, 1900

Loch Migdale

Much to my wife's distaste,
I've a weakness for short-cuts
that are nothing of the kind.
Like the one my family took

through the glen above Loch
Migdale, its single track at first
shaded by hazel woods, before
the view opened up of loch

and rust-roofed crofts. If fine,
we'd stop at the loch-end
and walk its length, taking in
the birch breath. I remember,

with my mother in old age,
strolling the two miles slowly,
while I waved a fern above her
to keep off clouds of midges.

BARTHOLOMEW MAP TITLE
*Life Insurance Map Showing
Extra Premiums for Residence
in Various Countries,* 1900

FLIGHT

'The truest literature in a stateless nation is that which maps the land.'
GAVIN WALLACE

Gavin, it's a beautiful winter's day –
East coast, clear and bright. Let's leave it there,
rinsed of all metaphors. Instead, let's take a novel
for a walk – a good long, meandering walk.

Let the novel be contemporary, Scottish,
and let's love it; let's love its good writing,
before we even begin to discuss whatever
it is that makes it so. This is buoying us up

and, with each step, we're joined by others,
sharing in your generosity and insight. And you're
leaning into your laugh now – that splutter
of delight – as you dance over the pages

filling them with possibility and light. Gavin,
love gives us flight. Let's all of us
take off, fly over the blue dashing Forth.
Let's circle Fife – its harbours, its gentle fields,

its friendly, sociable commute. It's late, Gavin.
We love you, Gavin. But we're losing height.
One last hug; one final, fulsome kiss, cheek to cheek.
And we head for home, each of us diminished.

BARTHOLOMEW MAP TITLE

A Map to Illustrate R. L. Stevenson's
Life in the South Seas, 1901

CONCERNING THE ATLAS
OF SCOTLAND

Joan Blaeu to Sir John Scot of Scotstarvit, 1642

When I learned that your Lordship
      had shown to his Royal Majesty,
on Charles I's unhappy visit to Scotland,
      the proofs of maps, previously sent
by me to be corrected, I wondered

what he could have made of them.
      Much in them was held in suspense,
as is the case in these fresher efforts, which,
      though a little tidier, still lack,
for perfection's sake, ornaments, titles,

distances and other such matters. For
      embellishment, I should be greatly
assisted by knowledge of the advantages
      of each region. That is to say, what crops
each produces, what metals it has,

what animals it bears or nourishes
      and so on. I ask this, for much
presents itself to people living there
      which is less obvious to me, who must
rely, in this whole enterprise, on

the tongues and hands of many men
        never met in their own domicile
or here in Amsterdam. It is over
        twenty years since, for the common
good of your Lordship's country

and of the commonwealth of literature,
        my father began, with you, to pull
from darkness the first atlas of your land.
        My father planned this – the fifth volume
of his geographical theatre – as a service

to posterity. Yet we are still wanting
        many maps. Among them: Sutherland,
Strathleith, Assynt, Ross, Lochaber and Lorne.
        Would that some hope remained
of uncovering these, for the Scotland

we wish to deliver is not one that
        shadows envelop, but one lit
and gleaming in all its parts. So too
        we desire the delineations of cities
and the sitings of all castles of note.

Most necessary of all are the arms
        or bearings with the names of Dukes,
Earls or Barons or other illustrious men –
        those whom you judge it expedient
that we inscribe on our fine copper plates.

These would add splendour to the maps
        and to descriptions of the genealogy
of those with a distinguished lineage.
        (On such depends the furtherance
of all our plans.) We have moved far

N
14 ← → 15

in troubled times; firm in the belief
        our colours will long outlast them.
The fractured depictions with which we began,
        the blanks which were without utterance,
are being addressed. We have recovered

much of what was lost; we have given
        shape and polish to what had been deformed.
Soon, the Scotland that had been partial
        will emerge into full, clear light. For that,
I await the corrections I have outlined.

BARTHOLOMEW MAP TITLE
Our corner of China, 1893

P A R S

Wynebrughlaw
Cornley
Kenmoir
Skioch
Skarr
Strontwhonn
Hoome
Skinfurt
Speddochs
Birkbuß
Dyum
Mill

L. Ruttann
Drumjowan
Beltanhill
Barnshouill
The Rowtan bridge
Vnderwood
Neu mill
Cleuchbrae
Coloc hen
Sleng
byr
Moriſton
Nunland
Steelſto
un
Stronchreigan
Fourmarkland
Tour
Gribtoun
K. of
Torregills
Torregills Caſt.
Glen mills
Hal o myir
Corruckan
Torachtytoun
Toregillstoun
Barnhill
N. Gribtoun
K. of Dunſkoir
Buß Kirkſmiell
Greinmeß
Torachty
Starriheuch
Garrach
Creuſtoun
Mill
N. Gribtoun
Kephall
Kargann R.
Ridbra
K. of Iracuyir
Neutoun
Colledge of Linclou
Clenry
Vle
Nyth flu.
Bilbow
Brigend
Harthorn
den
Killyburn
Halywod od K.
Halywood
Couhill
Portrac
Glenhowen
Glen kapill
N. Bourlands
Mid. bourlan
Bourlands
Kaltoun
Kelrountoun
Netherwood
Mill
Spittell
Caſtel Dykes
Mill of Deskonn
Hoome
Dun
ca
Bowes
Conhett
Carnſallach
Carryill
Q
Carlavereck
Shirringtoun
K. of Carl
Drumfrees
K. Maho
Blackshaw
Launes
Bunken
Lochyrr R.
The Vle
Reddingwood
Hemisfeeld
Caſteltoun
Deskon B.
Achincairn
Hempsfiell or Amisfeeld
Tyndell

A N N A N D I Æ

Damhead

Part   of   Anna

A BARTHOLOMEW'S DAY OUT

*Souvenir of the 10th Annual Picnic of the Employees of the Edinburgh
Geographical Institute. Snap Shots Taken at Elie. Saturday 24th June 1899.*

From Granton to Elie, all take to the deck,
imbibers of good salt air. Time has bathed
each of them in an even russet light.

A day calm enough for finery – hips
sleeved in elegant dresses, a bloom of capes,
hats extravagantly bowed. Even men

affect beribboned boaters. Their bearing
erect, their hands idle (for once); they talk
over the heads of boys privileged to be

within their circle. The youngest children
sit between the grown-ups, their Sunday hands
meekly in their laps. A man hoists his son

up the boat rail, the boy one rung up, heels
bracing his legs in place. The frayed feather
of his Glengarry brushes his father's

cap; he bent over his son, face so close
to his – oh, the sweet heat of a young son's
breath. This, then, is the spontaneity

of the snap. To their left, leaning side-on
to the rail – with broad back, flat cap, the blind
tip of a waxed moustache – it could be my

own grandfather, staring into the rest
of his life; if he had been a printer,
not a proud seaman who'd seen the world.

To his left, no more than a stride away,
as oblivious to father and son
as to the chance opprobrium of age,

a boy, whose broad white collar tops
an elegant knickerbocker suit, holds
that unmistakable stance – the legs

set wide apart, the curve of the arms
directed to a single point. As his friend
pats his privates back into place, this youth –

framed on the works day out – adds to the glint
of a watery map of Australia,
taking shape, like a dream, between his feet.

BARTHOLOMEW MAP TITLE
*Approximate Sketch Map of
Mean Annual Sunshine of
the British Isles,* 1893

THE ENGRAVER

Four months I'd spend, bent over
a sheet of copper, 2 feet by 2, glinting
like a coal scuttle on my worktop:

the engraver's task, to inscribe there
the reverse image of a map.

Always, I worked away from the body,
pushing thin threads through the metal.
I was tight-in as a dog on a trail.

Where I began, I soon forgot.
Where I'll end, you'll never know.
(This map too keeps its secrets.)

In time, a density of effects formed
below my blind hand. Few will be as intimate
with its contours as I was; or with the wilfulness

of a river, its horseshoe turns, its hidden
gullies through the marked fields.
I followed wherever it went: a nib, a beak,
                              a blade on the ice.

I tracked the (inverted) poetry of place.

Yet there came a time,
when I'd lift my head –
not godlike or summit-sure –

but almost casually,
in the way of someone lost
in a book on a speeding train.

He glances up – on an evening
when a coppery light slants
across the sky –

to see the landscape unfold
before him; lay itself out
without guile.

He can read its familiar fields, its farms,
the sailing boat on the molten river

which reminds him of a dhow
he once saw engraved in a silent world

the breeze tipping its sail, gently,
towards the water.

BARTHOLOMEW MAP TITLE

*Map of the Country of
the Arabian Horse,* 1894

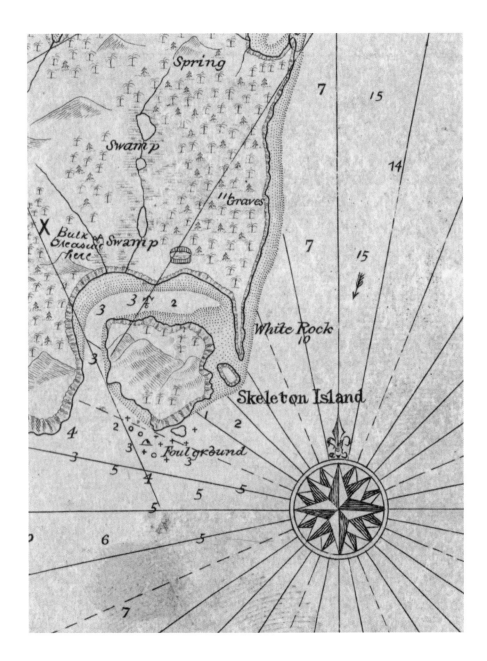

TREASURE ISLAND

Whether it was all by his own hand
or come across partially completed
by another

with a few strokes it became his
and always had been so.

He felt he could be drawing it in the sand
with a long stick, so sure was his hold
on its shape

or with a finger
daubing it out with mud or clay.
He marvelled at each gesture, how each

mark became
what it designated; and so

coves, rocks, hills and forests
formed spontaneously in his mind
as they were born upon the map.

Harbours pleased him like sonnets.

He dreamed he'd drawn
the map before and watched
with interest as his long, thin fingers
placed there

three crosses – two
in the north, one in the south –
with utmost assurance. But then

he'd seen the map
all his life – on the shadows
of the sick room wall,
on light playing through leaves.

And a story sprang from it now –
as it had on every other occasion.

Of course, the map had to be lost!

The foot had to brush it
from the sand; the careless hand
devour it. For the imprint

is never the imagination,
netting pictures, voices
and shadows, massing, shimmering

and holding off; holding off
till the moment is perfect.

Thereafter, the re-enactment.

He summons
cartographer and engraver.
He picks over the bones of his story,
so that the story may begin.

BARTHOLOMEW MAP TITLE
General Plan of the Central
& Eastern Portions of the
Witwatersrand Gold Fields, 1895

THE PRINCE OF CARTOGRAPHERS

John George Bartholomew 1860–1920 –
HIS JOURNAL – 'A General Chronicle'.

In tight black lines, barely
a legible pulse,

he maps his life,
till he arrives – like

a traveller in the souk
or a king at his court –

in the thick of it.
But first, aged 5,

he recalls: 'drowning
mice caught in a trap',

'bathing'; 'a blue
paint tin' – this last,

in the whole journal,
the sole icon. 'Rabbits

stolen' ('67);
then, in '79,

something darker:
'dissatisfied with life,

moustache
beginning to grow.'

(All his life he'll fight
melancholia –

like RLS,
travel for his health.)

April 1889,
underlined in red,

'married
Jennie Macdonald.'

The following, 'a year
of much work

and happiness.'
The Work column writhes now

with print runs and sales.
Each month has the look

whole years once had.
Even so, lists – Work

in Hand (all ticked) – tumble
from the pages: maps,

atlases. Honours.
In the Journal, People

Met has replaced Friends:
the shy man begins

to self-armour.
1910 (aged 50):

his portrait is painted
by E. A. Walton

(R. S. A.). Walton
catches John George's

confident gaze (the fine-
ness of beard and 'tache).

He wears the red robes
of authority, long-

fingered right hand
resting on the globe.

He is secure in his
dynasty, in what

he has inherited
and in what will pass

N
28 ← → 29

from him – a legacy
of science and industry:

not only (Hon) Doctor
of Laws, but a 'Prince

among Cartographers'.
Diego Velasquez

gave Philip IV
the same calm assurance –

Philip, a man who also
liked to keep a hand

firmly on the tiller.
J. M. Barrie (same age)

was also honoured
that day, though for other

kinds of mapping: 'Second
star to the right and

straight on 'til morning.'
1916: John George's

son, Hugh, is killed in France.
The rest of the journal –

lightly pencilled dates,
blank pages, mourning.

BARTHOLOMEW MAP TITLE
The Automobile Association
Telephone Box Location Map of
England, Wales & Scotland, 1942

Directions for Drawing Europe

1. Draw a straight line **AA** from North Cape to Cape Matapan.
2. From North Cape draw the straight line **E** at right angles to **AA**.
3. From Cape Stadtland draw the line **D** parallel to **E**.
4. From the mouth of the Weser draw **CC** parallel to **D**.
5. From Cape Apsheron draw the line **B** parallel to **CC**.
6. Draw a straight line from North Cape to Cape Stadtland.
7. Draw a straight line from Cape Stadtland to the mouth of the Weser.
8. Draw a straight line from the mouth of the Weser to Cape Finisterre.
9. Another straight line from Cape Finisterre to Gibraltar.
10. A straight line from Gibraltar to Genoa.
11. A straight line from Genoa to Cape Matapan.
12. A straight line from Cape Matapan to the Crimea.
13. A straight line from the Cape Apsheron to Kara Bay.
14. A straight line from Kara Bay to the mouth of the Mezene.
15. A straight line from the mouth of the Mezene to the North Cape.

FOOTNOTE

At the International Geographical Congress in Berne in 1891, it was felt that the great age of exploration was coming to an end. The time was right to consolidate the knowledge gained by producing the International Map of the World. The several agencies that the production depended upon would, through co-operation, demonstrate the universality of the project. That the map was never produced does not surprise us, but nor does it mean that the map does not exist. It survives as a series of intentional co-ordinates on which we can reflect; in the way that Jorge Luis Borges did on certain 'texts' that had no existence beyond his commentary upon them. I would refer most particularly to his A Universal History of Infamy, in which, "The College of Cartographers evolved a Map of the Empire that was of the same scale as the Empire and that coincided with it point for point." Whatever the circumstances that gave rise to the possibility of the Map of the World, they clearly never arose again. In fact, the millions of dead, which were to be a feature of the following century, spoke with one voice that the idea was a folly. Does technology suggest though that such a map is a living possibility, one free from ideology and meaning, now that the world itself has become the map; and the map a remorseless consumer of the world?

BARTHOLOMEW MAP TITLE

New plan of Glasgow with suburbs, by John Bartholomew, issued by the Glasgow United Young Men`s Christian Association showing the distribution of Public Houses, Licensed Grocers, Churches, and Branches of the "G.U.Y.M.C.A", 1884

COMPILATION

The aeroplane photos are particularly good
in this part of the line. The ground is chalky
and the trenches show up clearly –

as if the land has been overlaid
by a halting, runaway stitch.

Beneath such raw insistence,
surfacing from a subtler time, the fields
are laid out like faded flags –

each one pocked with shell holes. In one
aerial photo, someone's marked in
what once was

    a railway, a village, a town

(though the lens is too distant
to document the intimacy of destruction:

a piano disem-
    bowelled in the village street

the shell-like glint of crockery
    smashed by a careless tide

the fruit trees in *les jardins* cut down,
      wantonly, with an axe)

           *

Even more useful to know, of course,
would be which of these trenches Death has emptied
and which contain impending Death.

           *

I never yet thanked you for the lemons you sent.
They were enjoyed by several others besides myself.
There was only one casualty in the whole box.

BARTHOLOMEW MAP TITLE
Map of Edinburgh showing distribution
of cases of pulmonary tuberculosis
received at the Victoria Dispensary for
Consumption and Diseases of the Chest
during three years, 1892

THE MAPMAKER'S SON

Do you remember, when we were children
at Falcon Hall, the huge autumn bonfires
Daddie used to organise? Six feet high
or more, some of the branches we dragged there –
far taller than we were! How the flames leapt –

three times higher yet and, when the red logs
sank, we beat them with our sticks till the clouds
of sparks rose up so high, they were lost
among the pale young stars that were the first
to show. I can still taste the potatoes

we pulled black from the embers, the salt poured
from the torn corner of a paper poke.
Our Company's in Support now, camped
in a large oak forest. In a clearing,
there's a fine blazing fire and around it

all of the men companionably sit
listening to a song or joining in
the chorus. Briefly, they're free from the plagues:
the mud, the biblical frogs, the beetles
that infest the trenches. The firelight

freshens their tired faces, as once it did,
less deceitfully, ours; and the sweet smell
of burning wood – layered with memory –
brings out the stories, in the way it did
with Daddie. And, like Daddie, we all try

to bring the promise of adventure close.
There are many with us from foreign lands
and the more I hear their stories, the more
I want to travel, once war is over.
But to take my time, working my passage

from place to place – the veldt of Africa;
South America, California –
not as a tourist, but getting to know
the people and their ways. Some of the men
prefer to sleep beside the dying fire

than return to their tents; there, they can let
the stories live that little bit longer.
But we officers have a Nissen Hut –
and a splendid summer house it would make,
I've decided, once all this is over.

Every time wind rustles the trees, acorns
rattle on its iron roof, to remind us
autumn's here and winter not far off.

THE ESCAPE HANDKERCHIEF

When I first went to war,
      my true love gave to me
a handkerchief should I be lost
      so far across the sea.

It was a magic hankie:
      the map upon it changed –
whichever war I fought in,
      this map found its range.

No matter where they sent me
      behind the enemy's lines,
I mapped a route back to her heart
      past wire, guns and mines.

But now the map is bloody,
        so many wars it's seen.
My love takes it to the fountain;
        she never gets it clean.

Yet while wars continue,
        my true love must press on me
a handkerchief should I be lost
        so far across the sea.

But all things lose their magic –
        no map shows the route I took;
my body scattered far and wide
        as the ashes of a book.

BARTHOLOMEW MAP TITLE
Glasgow Corporation (sewage).
Map showing the situation and
the surroundings of the
Glasgow sewage works, 1904

THE MYTHO-MAP OF SCOTLAND

It was a day of sleet and hail. Nothing doing. They'd never seen their country bigger than a tea towel, so Diarmid suggested they make, with their friends, the biggest map of Scotland ever seen. They cleared the old ballroom and sent out for cured hides – sixty at least - of sheep, cattle, deer and goat. They would be pinned with the fine bones of herring, sewed with sinews from road-kill. They wanted the map, in important ways, *to be* Scotland: its contours not only to be accurate, but the hills and the mountains to rise from its surface – to look as if the flat, hanging plain of the map would offer you footholds like a climbing wall. Each one of them worked on a segment – pillaged the garden for tinctures of bark, moss and root – yet between them they shared a common mind, so that, when the pieces were joined with the translucent herring bones and sewn into place, there was no pause in the flow of a river, no break in the rise and fall of many mountains. The map reared like a mythical animal – you could easily think it might roar. But hold on! What's this? Along one flank you spot a weakness.

In the west, the green bleeds out into whiteness: the scattered villages remain, each one carefully named – but now frozen in abandonment; each peninsula is brushed by its own chill fjord. Some nuclear winter has passed here for which all were unprepared. And then, in the east, along one stretch, the care has been suspended, the pure intentions laid aside. At its midriff, two sides of the same blue firth cross each other like a twisted intestine. And look how crudely these other blue arteries run. Where can that pink umbilical cord be going for a walk? It seems either playfulness or wilfulness could no longer be denied. The roar of the map is from the wounds it bears; from a lack of care that renders it both magnificent and ruined. So many questions are embedded in its heart. Meanwhile, a cold sunlight has brushed the hail away. The pavements shine like a licked pencil. In the distance, the soft Pentlands come close as if you could take one in the palm of your hand and pull yourself there; as if they're saying, *Step outside, we're waiting.*

13 / 23

- -

BARTHOLOMEW MAP TITLE

Map showing the stepping stones across the Atlantic with insects of the Faeroes and Iceland, 1941

SILENCES

'…that which is absent from maps is as much a proper field
for enquiry as that which is present.'
J. B. HARLEY

This is not a horse.
Though if you were to listen hard,
you could smell the herd.

*

This is not a shoal
of fish. This is not silver
that's shifting, but light.

*

This is not a church.
This is a flustered sparrow
in a cage of straw.

*

This is not a map.
This is my voice, passing through
a field of ripe wheat.

*

No, this is not a
mountain. This is memory
waiting for your boots.

BARTHOLOMEW MAP TITLE
*Cape Colony showing the
distribution of goats,* 1902

THE MAP

More delicate than the historians'
*   are the map-makers' colors.*
ELIZABETH BISHOP

So plain is your Map, yet so guarded, perhaps
the whole poem's to be read aslant.
For, taken as it stands, it's hard to see

how the map-maker can draw without
the other's assent: there's no innocence
even in the idlest musings on a map.

To mark out space is simply the first step
in controlling what takes place within
its borders. No matter what colour

a country may choose, another's fiction
may drench it in blood. Our times,
in this, allow for little latitude:

The territory does not survive
the map. And though pretty colours can be
diverting, they hide what's most dangerous

of all: to lack colour altogether.
Terra Nullius. In the white brackets
of the map, where no titled landowner lives,

there shall you know the map-maker, of which
Bishop speaks, best of all. For where the
silences lie is always the test;

and the stories are still to be written –
even as satellites circle – of how
the powerless find their places on the map.

BARTHOLOMEW MAP TITLE
*Plan of City of Birmingham showing
fatal street accidents due to vehicular
traffic for the year ended 31st
December 1938, 1939*

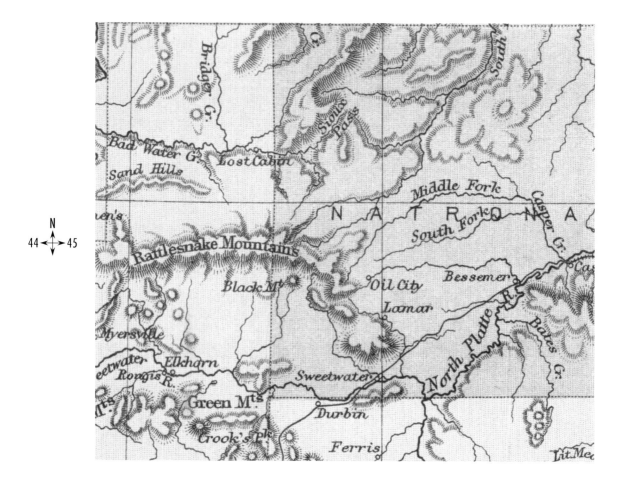

IN THE MAP ARCHIVE

At times, in the map archive, before the lights
(on a time lapse) return me to the tomb,
I love to tug at the broad metal drawers
and to peer into worlds teeming as rock pools.

In one drawer, I discover early India
in pen and ink, its place names already dense
as a seaweed's tangled fronds. In another
there's a shoal of maps from World War One,

their skin a robust if musty linen.
Trenches and front lines lap across them,
net the shifting points of a million deaths.
One drawer, I term Discovery, harbours,

among stacks of torn folders, a paper-clipped
swatch of tobacco-coloured stubs –
the tiny perfections of Rona, Staffa
and St. Kilda, alone in the waxy sea.

But in the others – let's call them Industry –
each map is a revision, is corrections,
is notes in the margin, circles and arrows,
telling us this is what we were, not the way

the tireless world is now. Maps archive
our appetites: railways, roads, airports –
mark them, number them, reroute them.
How can we not love such energy and enterprise?

Yet no amount of labelling will turn
a space into a place, unless memories
are aligned there. Even when I cross
the grey vault to visit distant drawers,

seeking a faint green spectra of air,
sky and light – Wyoming or Montana, places
where much is crudely named Well, Creek, Ranch,
Hollow – I am moved by the residues

of human longing to be found there.
But too soon the lights go out. The drawer clicks shut.
I'm still on westward tracks, as I feel my way
between silent stacks, mapless in the dark.

N
46 ←→ 47

BARTHOLOMEW MAP TITLE
*Map to illustrate extension of range
of the Capercaillie in Scotland since
its restoration at Taymouth
in 1837–1838, 1879*

MOTORING

b. 1950, I lived through the last years
of motoring. On a weekend, we'd take
a drive, two hours from Edinburgh,

in the Standard Vanguard that doubled
as a blunt-nosed tank. Always there'd be
a book of the road; and always a rug.

At journey's end, there'd be a picnic too
or, if the time was right, afternoon tea.
To get 'a bit of a blow' was the thing –

to walk through a forest, to breathe sea air,
to climb a knoll with a view. But motoring
was about more than getting from A to B.

It was about dawdling, looking, smelling
at speed; it was about indecision
as much as about mastery of the map.

The Touring Map ads tell us, in clear lines,
of once-upon-a-time when motorist
and hiker were both tweedy wayfarers

in a classless pre-war world. See how they
consult the map together, as the car
idles on the empty road. One year,

we drove north after a holiday down south.
Leaving such a world (tiny roads threading
through villages and village greens),

we drilled through the dead centre of England;
through limestone, through shale, through coal that crumbled
to dust. Huddersfield, Halifax –

we stared out at grey hills, at grey dykes,
at grass coated in ash. Sheep like stones.
Our beating hearts felt delicate, at risk.

Pity who has to live here, we each said
in our different ways. We were heading
for Haworth, a pilgrimage of sorts,

though only because Haworth was close
to our route. Our mother had long been in thrall
to all the Brontës, their undisclosed

intimacy, their lonely, unhappy
lives. Mum's had been a sickly childhood –
the parsonage spoke to her of confinement,

the moors of what couldn't be tracked or mapped.
We paid our visit, we read the labels;
we walked around the dour, oppressive streets.

Mum said she sensed the moors. I can't recall
any more of that trip, beyond these fields
of grim passion, surrounded by grime.

That's what the joy of motoring could yield.

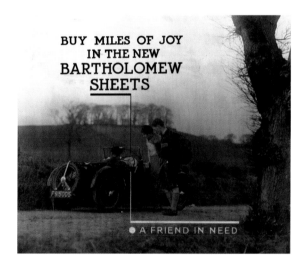

BARTHOLOMEW MAP TITLE
*Crawford's War Map presented
by the proprietors of Crawford's
Biscuits,* 1914

THE COLOURISTS

I think the name kind o confuses folk.
Everybody thinks you coloured in maps
and we didn't. We used a brown gunge
to paint a shape that blocked out the light –
one for each of the six colours. Each time
the glass plate was cleaned and another shape
added. It was delicate, skilled work we did –
and Bartholomew's was good to work for.
But sometimes, to me, it felt jist like school,
it was that strict! We weren't allowed to talk,
only to sing. *She loves you, yeah, yeah, yeah!*
Ba ba ba ba barbara ann. Some summers,
with these high windows, it'd be so hot –
as close to Beach-Boys-hot as we thought
we'd ever get. And it was such fine work,
you'd be staring from six inches away
at this glass plate, lit by bulbs from below.
More than once, my head crashed on the glass.
But then, come winter, unless you bagged
a table near a heater, it got cold; so cold,
one of the old biddies tied cardboard splints
round her legs to keep warm. You could aye
hear her coming! But Ida – she was the one
watched over us. She sat at her table, peeling
grapes or breaking apart twenty ciggies

to roll them into twenty-five. Weird, that's what
she was. But you had to do what you were told
in these days. We'd set times to go to the toilet.
You'd watch that hand creep up the clock –
tick tick tick tock. Aye, and as apprentices,
we'd to go messages, to the drawing office
and so on. We were a roomful of girls, so,
out in the factory, yer wee heart would be
fluttering, even though the men said teasing
was only a bit o banter. It was the '60s, though,
and you wore a little mini-skirt that didn't even
cover your bum. And spinster Ida was no help.
She'd come up to you – skinny wee thing
that you were – and say, 'God, you've no bust!
I always had a good bust!' And you were so shy
and timid you jist accepted it. A sign o the times.
Jist like when you walked through the printers'
and the machine room and the men were like,
'Can you get me this? Can you get me that?'
Before you know it, you've a shopping bag to fill.
I got a couple o dates for the Christmas dance
out of it, but they didn't come to much. In fact,
the most fun we had was watching men sprint
along the long corridor, practising for the sports.
Eventually, I did leave to start a family. The sky
was blue over Arthur Seat and my heart leapt
a little, like I was leaving school for a second time.

But Bartholomew's was a good firm to work for
and I was proud o the work I did there. You never
had any fears, once a map was completed,
that there was going to be anything wrong with it.
For all that the high stools gave me a sore bum,
I was happy there. To be honest, I still dream
endless times about being back in the colourists.

BARTHOLOMEW MAP TITLE

*Distribution of Drunkenness in
England & Wales,* 1902

THE SOVIET MAP OF EDINBURGH

In the summer of '68, my last year,
every Friday a few of us took to skiving off
at lunchtime. No one noticed. We saw the city
gleam from Arthur Seat or we prised our blazers
through two bent bars and strolled with gazelles
on the high, dry plains of the zoo. And Cramond Island? –
most who walked that wet mile – the young drinkers,
the heavy petters – missed many a tide
in the oncoming of another one. Not us.

We weren't exactly mapping the city,
but there was an unsaid sense of testing
its possibilities – or of saying a drawn out goodbye.
I can't recall ever being watched from afar
or engaged in idle chatter by strangers
with thick accents, schooled in charm;
though I'd have thought (mistakenly)
our destinations would hold their interest.
Even then, it's said, they could drive a tank
straight to my door. Like a homing dog,

it speeds along Carrington Road, straight up
the Avenue. Ivan knows his route will work;
after all, someone on the ground's measured
the bridges, noted the camber of all the main roads.

He's guided by what's colour-coded: a sharp-edged
black for industrial plants, purple – admin;
for the military, a fatigued combat green.

The map I'm looking at now's been updated.
1983. I can see the shape of Edinburgh,
tucked against the Forth, washed over with
beige estates, orangey roads. But the blocky
Cyrillic alphabet estranges me most – I reel
above a landscape I thought I knew.
Yet there must have been a mapmaker – one of
the 40,000 – who, in some vast Moscow hangar,
imagined this map animated in the field.
Songs for the Party were muted now,
the storming of privilege a routine affair.
More likely, he'd see tanks rolling along Princes Street;
a rash of proscriptions; a secret police, sifted
from collaborator and believer alike; shadows
haunting every street corner. After which:
a grey haar that feels as if it'll never lift.

Before the Wall came down, the KGB ensured
each map of the Soviet Union, destined for common hands,
was wrong. On the tourist map of Moscow, only
the outline contours of the city are right.
It seems unfair that even a tank knew
the quickest way to my door, while I'm
left disorientated by this Soviet reading

of my own home town. I take my bearings
from 'Princes Street', then retrace my steps
through memory, street by street, recognising
not one of the names, till, at last, I plot

my way home – sand on school shoes –
to find the house has long been taken.

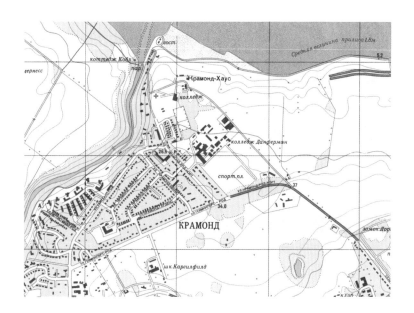

BARTHOLOMEW MAP TITLE
The Derbyshire Silica Fire Brick
Company's Friden Estate
& Workings, 1942

ORCHARD

An old map shows that,
where our terraced house
now stands, there was once

an orchard; neat rows
of prim pen and ink trees.
What fruit grew there

it doesn't say, but
on warm summer nights,
I hear ghost apples

pock the dry earth.
I smell the sweetness
of pears after rain.

BARTHOLOMEW MAP TITLE
The Eastern Mediterranean at
the Death of Herod Agrippa I.,
A.D. 44, 1900

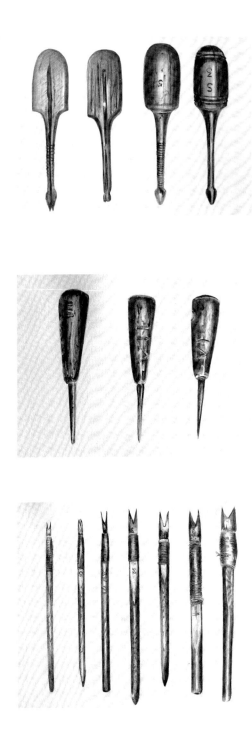

MAP MAN

For twenty years, Frank was my Map Man.
He'd arrive with his kitbag, map in hand, a spring

in every step. Of course we had our regular runs –
ones we could do almost blindfold. But, for the weekend,

something special. Frank laid the map on the table,
like it was the cover of a book, whose story you didn't yet know.

Trostan, Ae, Ettrick, Collochan, Shawhead, Glenkiln.
Now, see where these two roads meet? Yes, Frank, got you.

That's where we're going to park. We're going to run
up this track – there's an old farm up there. I'm reminded

of my love of old farms – the simple geometry of them,
the drama of the farmyard, how you feel it in each

of your senses: if it's quiet we'll run through the yard.
After the farm, the track narrows. Can you make it out?

Yes, it's a thread, it's the width of a running shoe. We're
running with sure-footed sheep, rabbits and deer. Great, Frank.

And sometimes, as you climb, because we're starting
to climb by now, you see buzzards. I see them already, right

Midrug

Ford

Larbreck

Skeoch

McNaughton

Fort

300

Drumclyer

Cro
Ho

400

Barnsoul

Well

500

Threepneuk

450

Crochmor

Holm Moor

Mill

Old Cluden

Crochmor

The Doons 284

ICK IRON GR

Knockshinnoch

400

Rosebank

Righead

idtown

Bush

Shawhead

319

352

T

325

Manse

Newmains

295

Burnside

Braco

Park

Bogrie Lane

Long Beech

329

Braco
Shed

Arnman

Little
Beech

292

300

300

roft
Romes
Beech

Bogrie

Merklands

350

12

279

Fore

head

305

Deanside

11

Barwhar

Bar

Brae

67

Bettyknowes

where Frank's finger is, circling above us. We've got to
keep moving! Now, says Frank, a hint of a smile more, it gets

really steep. My heart lunges at the contour lines,
narrowing ever further. Then, I think, great, Frank, let it

be steep, as steep as it likes. Sometimes, thigh muscles
need to ache before they can burn. And, once we're over

the top, there's a forest on the way down and this forest,
it's thick and it's dark and it's deep. And I'm thinking,

great, Frank, let the forest be dark, let it be deep, let it feel
as if we'll never get out of it. But already, I'm seeing us

bursting out of that darkness – we're the first flowers
of spring. Great, Frank. And then? Then it's a long way home –

and his finger describes a great arcing road back to the car.
Wow, that's far, Frank. But I'm thinking, Yes, be far – be

beyond my imagining; make it so far that the heart of this map
will bear our traces. Because, what we're going to do is

we're going to run – yes, Frank, yes, Frank, oh yes, Frank –
run till the landscape runs us. And the weather, Frank?

Unsure, might rain a bit. And I'm thinking, Rain –
we'll be in your face. Wind – we'll curse louder than you.

Sun – we'll be all over you. Snow, wind, hail and rain –
why thank you. You've just turned this into a Hero Run.

Great, Frank. All great. Except –
my ankle went two years ago now

just after we managed an old favourite
for Frank's seventieth. It was far from our longest run –

but it was a Hero Run for all that. I'm left
wondering now, whether, for cumulative happiness,

much has exceeded those map-planned runs with Frank.
Trostan, Ae, Ettrick, Collochan, Shawhead, Glenkiln.

Each name glows in its own firmament. And I think,
if God's house has many mansions, one of them

is surely papered with maps.

BARTHOLOMEW MAP TITLE
The Scottish Road Nook
Map of Scotland, 1937

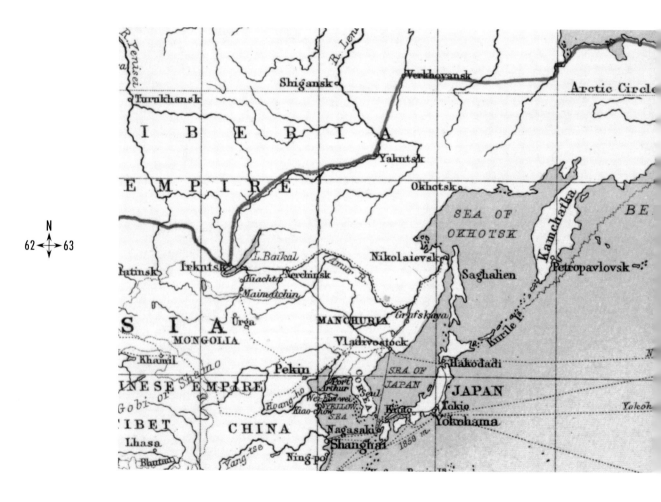

OLGA

1.

In the transportation season – those few months
when the northern passage isn't ice-locked –
      I sailed to Sakhalin on the Yaroslav
      from Odessa, by Suez and Vladivostock.

In our caged hold: eight hundred men, the dross
of European Russia; brute criminals
      of the most desperate kind. In with them,
      a seasoning of politicals –

conspirers against the state; men with sharp minds
and bloody intent. Over dinner, the captain told me
      how once, during a typhoon, he'd entered
      the hold. It had matched his vision of hell:

the howling of the gale, the searching heat, the cries
of terror from fettered wretches dreading death
      with each fresh crash of the sea. The harshest
      among them then considered his path.

Among such talk, you can imagine the pleasure
of having a pretty, dark-eyed girl share our meals
      in the wardroom; though Olga appeared
      ill at ease among the bearded, gold-tiered

officers of the Imperial Navy. For all
the uniformed grandeur, they lacked the grace
      to temper their conversation or their tales.
      Sometimes, she'd play the piano for us –

Cavalleria Rusticana or something
by Moskovsky or Glinka. But more often
      she'd refuse coffee, fold her napkin
      neatly and pass through us all like a fin

cuts through the sea. There was a moment's silence,
as each thought what he could have done to hold her.
      Then a toast was made and the roars began,
      as we covered the wake of her sadness.

One day, just past midnight, the air was motionless;
stars shone on the skin of the sea. The shadows
      of sentries were the only company,
      when I found myself, for the first time, close

and alone with Olga Elnikoff. I asked her
why she was the only woman travelling
      to this lonely spot. She answered my base
      Russian in purest French. Her case

was this: she was proceeding to Sakhalin
to be married. I imagined her intended
       to be some government bureaucrat
       who gave little thought to how delicate

she was; how harsh a penal colony would be
for the first years of their married life: but his thought
       was only for advancement. This was not
       so, she told me, her clear eyes fixed on mine.

Her intended was, instead, a young gentleman
in leg fetters with a shaven head. How her fate
       became one with his she would tell me,
       if I would care to hear. As the black snake

of Sakhalin roused itself from fog, Olga began.
Like many rich Russians, her parents had preferred
       to live anywhere but Russia. But she –
       a child with a studious mind – never cared

for the frivolous existences she observed
the emigrés live in Paris, Vienna or Rome.
       When her father died of typhoid one winter
       in Nice, Olga was far from unnerved

at immediate return to Russia to save
the last fragment of a shattered family fortune.
       They chose a university town
       where Olga could teach music and drawing.

Her students loved her and she prospered. Her life
seemed settled for a time. Then she met Serge Lepsky,
       a medical student, neither handsome
       nor rich, yet whose thoughtful conversation

beguiled her far more than the brainless chatter
of the aimless idlers she'd met in brighter times.
       Lepsky kept from her the slight matter
       of his anti-Tsarist beliefs –

he was already being watched by the police.
He was a man who'd given women little thought
       till now. But Olga's beauty, her devotion
       to her shamed mother, were revelations

to one who'd lived so long without connection
to his heart. Now, 'he fell in love with darkest wildwood,
       solitude, stillness and the night.'
       I watched Olga for a darkening of mood,

as she turned her eyes to the narrowing,
lightening sea. But then, on the becalmed water,
            a pair of whales swam by, shooting fountains
            into the air. I heard her small laughter.

2.

One morning in the summer of '93,
Olga took leave of her lover at the station.
            It was business, he said, that summoned him
            to Kieff: a lonely week without him.

But late one night, while the Elnikoffs were at supper,
he reappeared. Olga embraced him. (In Russia
            there are even brief journeys from which
            a traveller does not return.) He took some soup,

but he looked tired and restless, his neat dress dusty
and dishevelled. Olga had made the decision
            not to distress him with questions
            until what worried him had settled down.

He threw back a large glass of vodka; Olga played
Mendelssohn, as her mother, the Countess, sewed.
            There was a loud knock on the outer door.
            A confused murmur of voices was heard.

The women stared one to the other; and at Serge,
who they guessed was the heart of the matter. He held
        up a finger for silence. The clock ticked
        like a drum. In the stillness, Lepsky licked

his dry lips. 'Admittance in the name of the Tsar!'
It was only a moment's hesitation, and yet,
        within it, there was room for Lepsky's whole life
        to unfold. He walked slowly to the door.

He drew the bolts and the soft lamplight shone faintly
on the silver, yellow and black accoutrements
        of power. The dimly lit landing was crowded
        with men, one of whom Olga at once knew

was the Chief of Police. 'Serge Alexandrovich Lepsky,'
this man began, "I arrest you on suspicion
        of the murder of Otto Peltzer,
        in the province of Kieff on 9th June

of this year.' 'I did it,' said Lepsky quietly.
'He deserved to die.' Before they took him away,
        Olga was lost to her surroundings.
        This is a story composed of endings.

3.

The dark secret of the tragedy will be buried
with Lepsky and his wife on that lonely island
       in the Orkhovsk Sea. But the bones of it
       were laid bare at his trial. The papers

stitched the story and ran it daily. Peltzer
and Lepsky had been student friends. They'd set out
       for a day's fishing. But that evening
       Peltzer was found by the river, his throat

cut from ear to ear. Nothing had been taken from him.
Was the murder political or personal?
       We'll never know. But on whichever side
       betrayal lay, Olga never swayed.

Lifelong penal servitude on Sakhalin
was Lepsky's immoveable punishment. Thinking
       she might shield her mother from further shame,
       Olga insisted that her own name

be added to those sailing on the Yaroslav.
She would be permitted to marry convict Lepsky
       when the boat docked. Then, for five prison years,
       they must live apart. But, whatever years

were left, they must be lived on Sakhalin.
When the prisoners disembarked, Olga went below,
        to spare herself the sight of Serge in chains.
        They pulled him in a barge; before him

great fires, lit across the taiga, covered much of
the foreshore in smoke. This was their introduction
        to exile. This was where Olga's love
        had brought her. Serge wore a grey blanket drawn

round his shoulders. Fore and aft, his eyes searched her out.
For the weeks I was on Sakhalin, I saw
        meadows carpeted with wild flowers;
        and smelled the sweet scent of convict-mown hay.

70 ← ↕ → 71

But summer only lasts three months at the best;
the rest of the year, the island is ice-bound, the cold
        intense. I can almost smell that brief spring
        when I think of Olga and Serge, both old

before their time. Of all who sailed on that ship
of fools, it was Olga who deserved far better.
        I see her as Persephone, each year
        surfacing from darkness into hope

that love will shield them both in a prison
of their own making, rather than that other one –
    the ice-cold barbarous place they live in
    with its despair, its floggings and its chains.

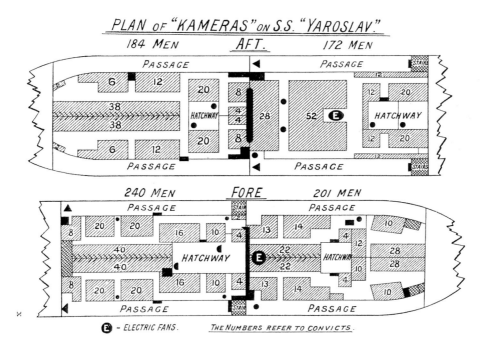

PLAN OF "KAMERAS" ON S.S. "YAROSLAV."

184 MEN   AFT.   172 MEN

PASSAGE   PASSAGE
6   12   20   8   12   20
38   HATCHWAY 4 28   52 E   HATCHWAY
38   4
6   12   20   8   12   20
PASSAGE   PASSAGE

240 MEN   FORE   201 MEN

PASSAGE   PASSAGE
8 20   20   16   10   4   13   14   10
   40   22   4 12   28
   40   HATCHWAY E   22   HATCHWAY   10   28
8 20   20   16   10   4   13   14   4   10
PASSAGE   PASSAGE

E = ELECTRIC FANS.   THE NUMBERS REFER TO CONVICTS.

BARTHOLOMEW MAP TITLE
*Ashworth: Anopheline Mosquitoes
in Scotland,* 1927

NOTES AND ACKNOWLEDGEMENTS

The poems in this book were written in response to experiences as the Bartholomew Writer in Residence at the National Library of Scotland, February–May 2013. Although Diane Garrick, the Artist in Residence, and I were given free rein within the NLS Maps Reading Room at Causewayside, the entry point and the primary focus of our work was the Bartholomew archive. The notes which follow are from Bartholomew Archivist, Karla Baker's exhibition descriptors – 'Putting Scotland on the Map, the World of John Bartholomew and Son' (NLS 7 Dec 2012-7 May 2013) – with additional contributions from Christopher Fleet, Senior Map Curator, NLS, and where appropriate, myself. Chris and Karla were also responsible for selecting the illustrative material in this book.

The Scottish printing and publishing house of John Bartholomew and Son Ltd was a map-making firm of world renown. From 1826 until 1995, Bartholomew produced maps for every occasion – from cycle touring maps to road atlases and school atlases to the 'Times Comprehensive Atlas of the World'. Behind the scenes, six generations of the Bartholomew family and hundreds of loyal and skilled craftsmen and women devoted their lives to the intricate processes involved in bringing Bartholomew's maps to life. Bartholomew focused the eyes of the world on Scotland as a centre of map-making excellence. It pushed the boundaries of what was possible and in so doing, has left a legacy that endures to this day.

A PAIR OF LOCHS
These lochs feature in The Bathymetrical Survey of Fresh Water Lochs of Scotland. This survey was the first comprehensive examination of the depths and nature of Scottish lochs. Between 1897 and 1907, Sir John Murray took 60,000 soundings of 562 major Scottish lakes. He went on to create detailed charts showing the depth of lochs. The Bathymetrical Survey was widely recognised at this time, placing Scotland at the forefront of organised lake studies (limnology).

FLIGHT

The epigraph by the late Gavin Wallace (1959-2013), Literature Director Scottish Arts Council/Creative Scotland, is his adaptation of a statement by Roderick Watson in his Edinburgh Companion to Scottish Literature: "The main 'state' left to a 'stateless nation' may well be its state of mind, and in that territory it is literature which maps the land." Gavin included it in an email to me on my appointment 11/12/12.

CONCERNING THE ATLAS OF SCOTLAND

This poem makes use of the letter from Joan Blaeu to Sir John Scot of Scotstarvit, dated March 1642, and from the Introduction to the Blaeu Atlas of Scotland itself. The letter from Blaeu to Scot forms one of 17 that survive today in the National Library of Scotland dating between 1626 and 1657. Most of the initial surveying work had been done by Timothy Pont in the late 16th century, but after Pont died, sometime before 1614, it was left to others to put his work into print. Sir John Scot of Scotstarvit promoted the publication process over 25 years, and also enlisted the help of Robert and James Gordon for writing geographical texts and improving upon the maps. Through the Blaeu Atlas, with its 47 regional maps of Scotland, and 154 pages of descriptive texts, Scotland became one of the best mapped countries in the world. The Blaeu Atlas provided the first, comprehensive mapping of Scotland, recording some 20,000 place names and other topographic features for the first time on sumptuous maps accompanied by flattering descriptions that promoted all the advantages of every region. By the 1660s, the Blaeu Atlas Maior had grown to 12 volumes and was the most expensive book money could buy, including nearly a whole volume devoted to maps of Scotland, and ensuring a wide awareness of Scotland across Europe, as well as the lasting survival of Pont's work in print for future generations.

A BARTHOLOMEW'S DAY OUT

To many, Bartholomew was a good employer, providing its staff with many benefits. Trips like the one to Elie gave staff the opportunity to dress up, have fun and play all sorts of games. Staff recalled spending weeks training for events in the corridors of Bartholomew's Park Road premises. The firm supplied refreshments and tried to ensure that a good time was had by all. Swimming seems to have been a particular feature of this trip. Annual dances, outings and picnics were complemented by a golf club and a staff share scheme. This scheme was ahead of its time and offered staff the right to hold shares in a firm to which many had devoted their entire working life.

THE ENGRAVER

Copperplate engravers required a steady hand. They were expected to be able to engrave very fine lettering and shapes onto a copperplate, in reverse. Engravers incised lines by working away from the body, rotating the copperplate as they worked. This meant they were not only working back to front, but often upside down too. Consequently, it took up to seven years to master this skill.

Engravers used a series of tools to produce different effects. Many of these tools were hand-made, using a variety of unexpected materials. Engraving points were made from recycled gramophone needles, shaped and sharpened to produce different effects. Line gauges were made out of flattened watch springs and their handles could be made from knitting needles or large tooth-picks from the butcher's shop.

The last major engraving project that Bartholomew completed was the five volumes of the Times Atlas of the World: Mid-Century Edition (1955–59).

TREASURE ISLAND

RLS's original map of Treasure Island was lost. He had to compose the map subsequently from information in the novel. He describes this as a dull process compared with drawing the map that gave him the story. The original copper book plate of Treasure Island is one of the most prized possessions in the NLS.

The line 'Harbours pleased him like sonnets' is adapted from an essay RLS wrote for The Idler (1894) concerning the drawing of the original map of Treasure Island: 'it contained harbours that pleased me like sonnets.'

THE PRINCE OF CARTOGRAPHERS

John George Bartholomew (1860–1920) was one of the most important figures in map-making at the turn of the last century. He believed that good maps and improved geographical teaching could benefit Scottish society in many different ways. He pushed the boundaries of what a map could be and he established one of Scotland's great institutions, the Royal Scottish Geographical Society.

What makes the achievements of John George Bartholomew even more remarkable is that they were won through adversity. John George suffered from ill health throughout his life, having contracted pulmonary tuberculosis in childhood. His symptoms included chest pain, severe coughing, weight loss and fatigue. He suffered from depression and his friends described him as being 'intensely shy' and 'diffident', or lacking in confidence. He was a very complex man, but, through sheer determination and a single-minded belief in the power of maps, he was able to overcome his difficulties and leave behind an enduring legacy.

COMPILATION
Compilation was one of the ways in which Bartholomew's kept their maps current. Newspapers were an important source of information to Bartholomew's draughtsmen, as were letters from cyclists on the state of roads. This poem borrows the method: it is drawn from the Log Book of G. H. F. Bartholomew (Hugh) Volume II, January 1, 1917 – June 9, 1917, subtitled, "Ye Historye of his adventures in ye Great Warre in ye Countrye of France in ye year 1917."

THE MAPMAKER'S SON
Drawn from memories of the childhood of George Hugh Freeland Bartholomew (Hugh), as written by his brothers and sisters, Ian, Betty, Bay and Maisie, and from letters from the Front. The letters were drawn from his last days there; the last letter was written on 22 September 1917. He was hit by shrapnel on 30 September and died on 2 October 1917, aged 21.

THE ESCAPE HANDKERCHIEF
In World Wars One and Two, and in subsequent wars, servicemen have been issued with handkerchiefs printed with the map of the country to which they were bound. The handkerchiefs could be easily carried and would help stranded servicemen to find their way to safety.

THE MYTHO-MAP OF SCOTLAND
'Bartholomew's Reduced Ordnance Survey Map of Scotland coloured to show orographical features' is is one of the biggest maps in the Bartholomew collection: every half-inch map of Scotland was pasted onto a linen backing and then hand-coloured. It has been impossible to reproduce, but the accompanying

'Tourist Map of Scotland' hand-coloured to depict "molehill-style" relief along the lines of 17th century or earlier maps, has a similarly pleasing animism.

THE MAP

This poem makes use of the following quotation: 'The territory no longer precedes the map, nor survives it. Henceforth, it is the map that precedes the territory.' Jean Baudrillard.

MOTORING

Bartholomew's was a popular map-maker. It stressed the reliability of its maps at a time when tourism – the adventure of the road – was opening up for both motorists and walkers. Advertising from the 1930s was clear, crisp and colourful. Many advertisements were unusual in the prominence given to women and in the use of photography. Bartholomew often used external studios to produce these posters.

THE COLOURISTS

The colourists – an all-female department – had one of the most technically challenging roles in the firm, as well as one of the most confusing titles. Colourists did not add the colour to the maps themselves, but rather they helped to build up the coloured areas of a map during the printing process. Bartholomew's maps could have up to eight different colours but early lithographic machines could only print one colour at a time. A colourist blocked out areas to make sure each colour was in the right place when the map was finished. This poem draws on a group interview of ex-colourists interviewed at the NLS in 2010 and on a chance encounter with a colourist at the Bartholomew exhibition.

THE SOVIET MAP OF EDINBURGH

'Every Soviet president, from Stalin to Gorbachev, and all high-ranking officers, knew not only where you lived but how to get there by tank. They knew the width of the roads, the height of the bridges, the depth of the rivers, the names of the streets. And they knew the exact location and purpose of every building of possible strategic importance, even those omitted from Ordnance Survey maps.' (from Uncle Joe Knew Where You Lived by John Davies.)

OLGA

Harry de Windt was a writer and adventurer. He made use of Bartholomew's maps in several of his books. *Olga* is based on an account in The New Siberia: A Visit to the Penal Island of Sakhalin, and Political Prison and Mines of the Trans-Baikal District, Eastern Siberia by Harry de Windt (London, Chapman and Hall, 1896). De Windt repeated the story in his autobiographical, My Restless Life with different dates. De Windt made the journey three years after Chekhov. Chekhov's account of the brutality of the floggings there, in The Island of Sakhalin (1893), helped to bring about the abolition of corporal punishment for women (in 1897) and for men (in 1904). The Yaroslav was built on the Clyde.

'he fell in love with darkest wildwood,
solitude, stillness and the night' is from *Eugene Onegin* by Pushkin.

A sincere thank you to Karla Baker, Beverley Casebow and Chris Fleet of the National Library for enthusiasm, insight and support during the residency and to Diane Garrick for accompanying me on the journey. My gratitude also to my agent, Jenny Brown, to Neville Moir and Jan Rutherford of Birlinn/Polygon, to Lois Wolffe of the NLS and to the designer Teresa Monachino (once again); and to Professor George Lovell for a crucial week of map-talk and *tapas* in Seville. It was George who taught me, over several *tintos*, that:

Ethnographers have no sense of time;
Historians even less about space.

One lot thinks everything's aye been;
The other couldn't fit a nose on a face.

That's why we need Geographers (oh yeah!) –
To tell us exactly where we are;

That's why we need Geographers (oh yeah!) –
To take us safely from bar to bar.

TOM POW *Dumfries 2014*
NX 966759 Lat / Lon: 55.067390, -3.6195867

A SELECTIVE BIBLIOGRAPHY OF RECENT MAP BOOKS

There are a large number of entertaining and informative books about mapping of which these are a few. All are available at the NLS Map Library at Causewayside.

Barber, Peter (ed), The Map Book, London: Weidenfeld and Nicolson, 2005

Bradshaw, Ross (ed), Maps, Nottingham: Five Leaves Publications, 2011

Coverley, Merlin, Psychogeography, Harpenden: Pocket Essentials, 2010

Fleet, Christopher; Wilkes, Margaret; Withers, Charles WJ, Scotland: Mapping the Nation, Edinburgh: Birlinn, 2011

Garfield, Simon, On The Map: Why the World Looks the Way It Does, London: Profile Books, 2012

Harman, Katherine, You Are Here: Personal Geographies and Other Maps of the Imagination, New York: Princeton Architectural Press, 2004

Harman, Katherine, The Map as Art: Contemporary Artists Explore Cartography, New York: Princeton Architectural Press, 2009

Hartley, JB, The New Nature of Maps: Essays in the History of Cartography (ed. Paul Laxton), Baltimore and London: John Hopkins University Press, 2001

Hewitt, Rachel, Map of a Nation: A Biography of the Ordnance Survey, London: Granta, 2010

Jennings, Ken, Maphead, New York: Scribner, 2011

Solnit, Rebecca, A Field Guide to Getting Lost, Edinburgh: Canongate Books, 2006

Turchi, Peter, Maps of the Imagination: The Writer as Cartographer, San Antonio: Trinity University Press, 2004

RELEVANT WEBSITES -

http://maps.nls.uk/ for Map Resources at the NLS.

http://www.maphistory.info/ 'Map History' website is a useful portal to history of cartography resources.

OldMapsOnline (http://www.oldmapsonline.org) is the largest portal to zoomable historical maps of the World.

Bartholomew's Archive – digital.nls.uk/bartholomew/

Duncan Street Explorer - a stand-alone, interactive, exhibition. http://digital.nls.uk/bartholomew/duncan-street-explorer/index.html.

For a complete facsimile of all the maps and texts from Bathymetrical Survey of the Freshwater Lochs of Scotland (1897-1909), http://maps.nls.uk/bathymetric/index.html

Blaeu Atlas of Scotland website: http://maps.nls.uk/atlas/blaeu/index.html (includes the History behind the publication of the Blaeu Atlas of Scotland for further detail and references: http://maps.nls.uk/atlas/blaeu/history_behind_publication.html)

LIST OF ILLUSTRATIONS

Page 4: Lettering sample by David Anderson, former apprentice draughtsman at John Bartholomew & Son, c 1950. Reproduced with kind permission of HarperCollins Publishers and the National Library of Scotland. Page 6: Lochs Ruthven & a' Choire. From: *Bathymetrical Survey of the Fresh-Water Lochs of Scotland*; constructed under the direction of Sir John Murray And Laurence Pullar during the years 1897 to 1909 (Vol. 4, Plate 105) [London] : Royal Geographical Society, surveyed 1903, published [1908]. Reproduced by permission of the National Library of Scotland. Page 15: Nithia Vicecomitatus, The Shirifdome of Nidis-dail, auctore Timotheo Pont. From: *Theatrum Orbis Terrarum sive Atlas Novus* (Vol. V) [Amsterdam : Blaeu, 1654]. Reproduced by permission of the National Library of Scotland. Page 20: Map of Treasure Island printed by John Bartholomew & Co., 28 March, 1895. Published in: *The Works of Robert Louis Stevenson. Romances, Volume I. Treasure Island.* [Edinburgh: Longmans Green and Co.; Cassell and Co.; Seeley and Co.; Chas. Scribner's Sons, 1895]. John Bartholomew & Co., 1895. Reproduced with kind permission of HarperCollins Publishers and the National Library of Scotland. Page 23: Spring divider. Page 24: An official portrait of John George Bartholomew (1860-1920) from the studio of London photographers Elliot and Fry, c 1900. Reproduced by permission of the National Library of Scotland. Page 30: Lessons in Map-Drawing by J. M. D. Meiklejohn, printed by John Bartholomew & Co., 5 September, 1912. Published in: *The Comparative Atlas Physical & Political by J. G. Bartholomew* [London: Meiklejohn

& Son, 1912]. John Bartholomew & Co., 1912. Reproduced with kind permission of HarperCollins Publishers and the National Library of Scotland. Page 39: Bartholomew's Reduced Ordnance Survey Map of Scotland hand-coloured to show orographical features, c 1910. Reproduced with kind permission of HarperCollins Publishers and the National Library of Scotland. Page 44: Wyoming, printed by John Bartholomew & Co., 7 January, 1893. Published in: *Chambers's Encyclopaedia: A Dictionary of Universal Knowledge, Vol. 10* [Philadelphia: J.B. Lippincott Company, 1893]. John Bartholomew & Co., 1893. Reproduced with kind permission of HarperCollins Publishers and the National Library of Scotland. Page 49: Bartholomew advertising, 'Buy Miles of Joy in the New Bartholomew Sheets', 1934. Reproduced with kind permission of HarperCollins Publishers and the National Library of Scotland. Page 52: Photograph of Bartholomew's colourists in their workshop at Duncan Street, Edinburgh, c 1960. Reproduced with kind permission of HarperCollins Publishers and the National Library of Scotland. Page 55: *Edinburg (N-30-6)* Russian Military Map (1983). Reproduced by permission of the National Library of Scotland. Page 57: Engraving tools. Page 59: Sheet 88 (Dumfries) from Ordnance Survey, One-Inch to the mile 'Popular' edition Scotland. [Southampton: Ordnance Survey, published 1925]. Reproduced by permission of the National Library of Scotland. Page 62: Arctic Coast Route from the Kolyma River to Bering Strait, printed by John Bartholomew & Co., 23 October, 1903. Published in: *From Paris to New York by Land* by Harry de Windt [London: George Newnes Ltd., 1904] John Bartholomew & Co., 1903. Reproduced with kind permission of HarperCollins Publishers and the National Library of Scotland.

BARTHOLOMEW MAP TITLE
Distribution of Lunacy Throughout the British Isles, 1902